D0014228

THE LITTLE HERB BOOK

Rosamond Richardson

PIATKUS

© 1988 Judy Piatkus (Publishers) Limited

First published in 1988 by
Judy Piatkus (Publishers) Limited,
5 Windmill Street, London W1P 1HF

Reprinted 1990

British Library Cataloguing in Publication Data
Richardson, Rosamond, *1945–*
The little herb book.
1. Herbs
I. Title
641.3'57

ISBN 0-86188-720-4

Drawings by Rosamond Richardson
Designed by Susan Ryall
Cover photograph by Theo Bergström

Phototypeset in 10 on 11pt Linotron Plantin by
Phoenix Photosetting, Chatham
Printed and bound in Great Britain by
The Bath Press, Avon

CONTENTS

HERBS IN HISTORY

Herbs have played an important role in everyday life for centuries – in cooking, in medicine, in aromatics and beauty care – and in other less ordinary aspects of life too: in superstition and magic, enchantment and religious ritual.

Perhaps the potency of herbs in magic and ritual derived from their highly effective medicinal uses. In early societies these natural healers came to be dedicated to the gods, and gradually legends were woven around particular plants and their associated deities. They were used in ceremonies both sacred and profane – equally to sanctify a temple or to invoke the Evil Eye.

The Egyptians used herbs to embalm the Pharaohs, and left herbs in their tombs to ensure a safe journey to the hereafter. The Greeks and Romans revered herbs and used them for incense in their worship: they decorated altars with them, wore them at weddings to bestow good luck, or strewed them at funerals to symbolize eternal life. The Greeks crowned the winners of their various games with bay, fennel and parsley, and the Romans presented worthy citizens and victorious warriors with herbal wreaths and crowns.

Both Greeks and Romans wore garlands of herbs at feasts and banquets, believing that by so doing they would avoid a hangover.

SOME HERBAL TRADITIONS

The Druids picked herbs with great reverence: dressed in white linen robes, with no shoes on, they cut especially precious herbs with a gold blade. It was considered most effective of all to pick herbs naked, at or just after the full moon.

Country folk had equal respect for herbs, since they were their medicine chest. The country wife, too, was careful how she picked them. She would always use her left hand, never cut with an iron tool, never face into the wind or look behind her whilst gathering. If she dropped her herbs on to the ground she believed that their strength leaked back into the earth. To the country wife a herb was not merely a cultivated culinary plant, it meant any number of the green plants that grew in the wild around her. These were the ones without a woody stem, so her lore applied to wild flowers and 'weeds' as much as to the well-known aromatic herbs that we use in cooking and aromatics today.

Ancient tradition decreed that all herbs should be sown or planted during the first or second quarter of the moon, and it was a small step from these superstitions to the place that herbs attained in the Middle Ages – in the magic artillery of witches' spells and potions. Herb garlands were hung on the door of a house on certain saints' days, and particular plants were believed to possess special powers to avert evil spirits, to protect the house from lightning, or to keep witches away. Many a cowherd would hang a bunch of herbs by the dairy door to stop the milk from turning sour, or prevent it being bewitched.

The 'Language of Flowers', evolved in early times by the Greeks, was closely connected with herbs and their powerful properties. It was a system of plant symbolism whereby every herb had a specific meaning – fidelity, doubt, pleasure or jealousy for example – and secret conversations could be conducted by exchanging posies or garlands. The tradition was passed on down through the centuries in Western Europe and became popular in medieval France. The Victorians revelled in it and many of the books on the 'Language of Flowers' date from this period.

HERBS IN MEDICINE

Man has always recognized the medicinal properties of herbs. Tablets found in the library of Assurbanipal, King of Assyria from 668–626 BC, show that his medical men were familiar with the properties of up to 250 plant drugs. In the heyday of classical Greece, Hippocrates (known as the 'Father of Modern Medicine') was the first man to separate demonology from medical practice, and among his 600 'simples' ('useful plants') are many remedies that we still use today.

The significance of the dual nature of herbs – as magic and medicine – culminated in Dioscorides' *De Materia Medica*, a work that closely influenced the great European herbals of the 16th and 17th centuries, when the famous trio of Turner, Gerard and Parkinson (and later the infamous Culpeper) rekindled a public awareness of herbs and their qualities.

Today, the unpredictable side-effects of synthetic drugs have led scientists to analyse plants with modern techniques, and their findings often verify traditional old wives' tales. The range of medicinal properties ascribed to herbs is very wide: many are both tonic and stimulant, a large number are sedative or digestive, are useful in chest conditions, or for gripes, flatulence, headaches or for skin conditions. Many were used for their antiseptic qualities – for cleansing open wounds and as disinfectants.

DRYING HERBS

To obtain maximum scent and flavour, herbs are best harvested just before they come into flower. Pick them on a sunny day, in the morning when any dew on them has dried, and lay them out on paper to dry in a warm place. Or you can hang them up in bunches in any airy place until the leaves are brittle. Then pull leaves off the stalks and store in dark glass containers. Keep herbs in a dark cool place and they will retain their fragrance for a longer time than if exposed to light and heat. Replace them annually.

INFUSIONS AND DECOCTIONS

To make an infusion, place ½ oz (15 g) dried herbs in a warm bowl, and pour over it 1 pint (600 ml) boiling water. For fresh herbs the ratio is 1 oz (30 g) to 1 pint (600 ml). Cover and leave for 10 minutes.

A decoction is made by soaking the dried herb in cold water for 10 minutes in an enamel saucepan. Bring to the boil, covered, and simmer for 2–3 minutes, then allow to steep for 10 minutes, still covered. Cool and strain.

For external use, a compress can be made by bringing 1–2 heaped tablespoons of the herb to the boil in 1 cup of water, covered. Steep for 5 minutes, still covered, then dip cotton wool into it and apply it to the lesion.

HERB GARDENING

The enchantment of a herb garden lies in the variety of foliage colour, the delightful flowers, and above all their aromas – which range from the sweetest imaginable to rancid and sour. Added to these joys, bees and butterflies are attracted to a herb garden.

Herbs lend themselves to garden design because they are hardy, quick growers, with luxuriant flowers. Some are evergreen, so a herb garden can look attractive all the year round, whether in a formal or an informal design. Herbs will grow on most soils and like a sunny position. Do not feed or over-water, just dead-head after flowering and leave them to rampage! Herbs grow successfully in borders, too, and can give a pretty cottage-garden effect.

Town dwellers can grow herbs in pots, window-boxes or tubs, so long as they have sun and good drainage. Grow from seed, or from cuttings, or buy young seedlings in early summer.

COOKING WITH HERBS

Herbs have taken their place in the greatest of the world's gastronomic dishes from East to West, North to South. Each one has its entirely individual flavour, and they are immensely versatile. They are a joy to cook with as they give an indefinable and special touch to whatever they are mixed with, and fill the kitchen with mouthwatering smells.

In general, dried herbs are far stronger than fresh ones, so smaller quantities are needed in cooking. Certainly some herbs dry better than others, and a few are better dried than fresh (bay and rosemary, for instance). The best herbs to use fresh in cooking are basil, borage, coriander, dill, fennel, tarragon, chives, tansy and parsley. Some herbs are as good dried as fresh – marigold, marjoram, mint, rosemary, sage and thyme – so these herbs can give gastronomic pleasure all year round.

Finely chopped or snipped herbs make beautiful soups and excellent sauces. They enhance stuffings for meat, pancakes and pastries, and roughly torn or chopped, they transform summer salads. Certain herbs have particular affinities – fennel with fish, rosemary with lamb, and so on – and some are delicious in desserts, mint and lemon balm for example.

BALM

Balm is a bee-plant, planted near orchards to attract bees, and bee-keepers used to rub the insides of their hives with lemon balm to encourage a new swarm to stay. Medicinally the herb has been used as a relaxant and was thought to be good for the heart – it relieved the anxiety and depression that brings on cardiac palpitations. Its essential oil contains citronella, and so has been useful as a wound herb. An early version of Eau de Cologne, *Eau de Carmes*, was distilled from balm leaves, and this aromatic herb makes a fragrant addition to summer salads and desserts.

BASIL

'Basil' comes from the Greek for a king, because the herb was used in ancient times as a royal unguent or medicine. Another story has it that it got its name from the fabled basilisk, the king of serpents said to be hatched by a snake from the egg of a cock. The legend goes that only a weasel was cunning enough to take it on in combat: this he did by eating the herb rue, which gave him such strength that he attacked and killed the monster. From then on it was said that basil and rue would not flourish in the same garden: the sweetest of herbs developed deep antipathy for the most bitter.

In India, basil is revered as sacred to the gods – even worshipped as a deity itself – and is invoked to protect all parts of the body. Yet, ambivalently, it was also dedicated to the Evil One, and is an emblem of hatred. In the Middle Ages it was believed that a sprig of basil laid under a pot would breed a scorpion; anyone who breathed in the scent of the herb would breed a scorpion in his brain, 'and after long and vehement pain he dies thereof'! Yet – another ambivalence – basil seeds were thought to *cure* the bites of scorpions.

Medicinally, basil is a tranquillizer and sedative, and infusions were prescribed for stomach cramps and sickness. It is a good digestive, stimulating the appetite as well as relieving constipation. It was said to be a cheering herb: Gerard said, 'Basil is good for the heart . . . . It taketh away sorrowfulness which commeth of melancholy and maketh a man merry and glad.'

Basil is a hot climate plant, cannot stand frost, and is therefore comparatively difficult to grow in northern climes. It can flourish, however, in greenhouses or as a pot plant. It needs light, well-drained soil and likes to be well watered in dry weather. It can grow to between 1 and 2 feet (30–60 cm) tall.

Basil is a fine culinary herb, and the principal ingredient of *pesto*, the inimitable sauce for pasta made with garlic, pine nuts, Parmesan cheese and olive oil. Basil goes particularly well with tomatoes, fish and chicken, is delicious with eggs, and was a traditional flavouring both for turtle soup and Fetter Lane sausages.

BASIL WITH TOMATOES AND MOZZARELLA

Fresh and summery, this aromatic dish makes a beautiful side vegetable to go with plain roast chicken or with steamed fish. I like to serve it as a starter sometimes, too – when basil is abundant and sun-ripened tomatoes are at their very best.

1 lb (500 g) tomatoes, sliced
8 oz (250 g) courgettes, very finely sliced
a medium bunch basil leaves, shredded
4 oz (100 g) Mozzarella cheese, sliced
salt and pepper
2 tablespoons grated Parmesan cheese
2 tablespoons dried breadcrumbs
a little olive oil

Make layers in an ovenproof dish with the sliced tomatoes, courgettes, basil and Mozzarella, seasoning with salt and pepper as you go. Mix the Parmesan with the breadcrumbs and sprinkle over the top. Dribble a little olive oil over the surface, and bake at 375°F/190°C/Gas 5 for 15 minutes. Serve piping hot.

Serves 4

BAY

The bay or sweet laurel tree was sacred to Apollo, god of music and poetry, prophecy and healing. Aesculapius, god of medicine, was traditionally crowned with a wreath of bay or laurel leaves, believed to be a panacea for all ills. An evergreen, bay became a symbol of eternity, but above all it represents glory. To the Romans a laurel wreath was a symbol of the highest achievement, the Greeks crowned the winner of the Pythian games with laurel, and the very word *laurels* has become synonymous with success. 'Baccalaureate' derives from *bacca lauri*, berried laurel, which in turn is the derivation of the term 'bachelor' (of an academic subject). Bay's culinary use is the flavouring of stocks, meat dishes, stews and casseroles. It is a vital ingredient of a *bouquet garni*, and it also lends a delicious flavour to barbecued foods.

BERGAMOT

A highly fragrant herb, bergamot attracts bees and its distinctive essential oil gives Earl Grey tea its aromatic flavour. It has been used in folk medicine to cure sore throats, colds and chest complaints, and an infusion of the leaves in hot milk makes a sedative nightcap. In the 19th century it was believed that bergamot tea increased fertility in young women, so a bergamot plant was sometimes included in their dowry. Bergamot leaves are a tasty addition to pork dishes, and the dramatic flowers make a spectacular decoration for a summer salad. Its essential oil is much used in perfumery.

In the old days bergamot was used to perfume starch. A 19th-century recipe goes: 'Stand some Bergamot and Lavender petals in Rose water all night and add the perfume so obtained to your starch, which you must make thicker than usual. This will give a nice perfume to linen.'

BORAGE

Borage is nature's 'happiness plant', and has been credited for centuries with raising the spirits of even the most melancholy. The ancient Greeks said that borage steeped in wine was a sure remedy for depression, and it is to this day added to a jug of

Pimms. Gerard quotes Pliny's epithet for the herb: 'I, Borage, bring alwaies courage.' So borage instils both happiness and courage, and also, according to Evelyn, 'sprigs of borage are of known virtue to revive the hypochondriac and cheer the hard student.'

Medicinally it was thought to be good for the blood, being rich in potassium and nitrate of potash, and in homoeopathic medicine a drug derived from borage is used to treat fevers and nervous disorders. Alfred the Great certainly knew it and referred to it as 'a maker of good blood'. A tisane of borage used to be prescribed for rheumatism and respiratory infections, and cooled a fever as well as calming delerium.

Borage leaves taste and smell rather like cucumber, and make a delicious soup. The bright cobalt blue flowers of this delightful herb are a stunning garnish for summer food. The soft, grey-green, hairy leaves can be cooked as a vegetable, like spinach, and lightly buttered – the Italians use this to stuff ravioli. The raw leaves are delicious in salads and sandwiches, and they make excellent fritters, cooked in light batter and eaten hot from the pan.

CHAMOMILE

Chamomile has a fragrant apple scent and got its name from the Greek for 'apple of the ground'. The Egyptians consecrated it to their gods, and it has been used in country medicine ever since. It was, however, a fairly rare plant in medieval England, brought into cultivation from the wild in about 1265 and planted in infirmary gardens. King Edward III's wardrobe accounts mention a purchase of chamomile to be used as a clothes freshener. By the 17th century chamomile was in regular use as a medicinal and beauty herb, and the Pilgrim Fathers took it with them to the New World. In the late 19th century it was grown in Mitcham, Surrey, alongside the famous Mitcham lavender, purely for its medicinal qualities.

The deep blue oil extracted from chamomile flowers contains azulene, an anti-inflammatory substance, used in poultices to reduce swellings.

Chamomile makes a soothing, healing eye lotion, and a good dressing for insect bites and stings. Infusions of chamomile alleviate stomach cramps and muscular spasms, and ease painful menstruation. It is a mild sedative, too, and chamomile tea is well known as a sedative and tonic drink, an effective nightcap which is also said to erase unlovely lines on the face.

Little sprigs of chamomile are a tasty addition to a salad, and give an original flavour to sauces and mayonnaise. Try the leaves chopped up in an omelette *fines herbes*, or mix them into bread dough as do traditional Provençal bakers. Chamomile is added to *manzanilla* sherry for its apple flavour, and in the Middle Ages, before the advent of the hop, the whole herb was used in the manufacture of beer.

Chamomile grows wild in meadows and grass verges and on the edge of woodland. It is a native of Southern Europe and thrives on waste ground and poor sandy soils. It likes moist, light soil and plenty of sun, and propagates fast by root runners. A chamomile lawn is a delight in a garden, its apple fragrance wafting up as you walk on it. 'The more it is trodden, the more it will spread,' maintains Falstaff in *Henry IV*. Plant it from seed, or with young plants set slightly apart. If you keep it lightly and regularly watered, and mown to about ½ inch in height, it will wear as well as grass.

Chamomile is a good 'companion' plant – it is known as 'the plants' physician' because if it is grown near sickly or unhealth plants of any kind, they recover.

CHAMOMILE HAIR RINSE

Pour 1 pint (600 ml) boiling water over 1 oz (25 g) chamomile leaves. Put into an enamel saucepan and heat gently. Bring to just below simmering point and heat for 10 minutes. Do not boil. Remove the pan from the heat and leave overnight.

Rub a few tablespoons of the strained rinse into the hair after shampooing, working it in well with the fingertips. Leave on the hair for 5–10 minutes before rinsing off thoroughly.

CHAMOMILE TEA

1 oz (25 g) fresh chamomile leaves
1 pint (600 ml) boiling water
honey (optional)

Strip the leaves off their stalks and put them into a medium sized teapot. Pour the boiling water over them, cover with the lid, and leave to stand for 5 minutes. Sweeten the tea with a teaspoon of honey if desired.

Serves 2

CHIVES

Chives belong to the onion family, and are closely related to leeks and garlic. Their botanical name is *Allium schoenoprasum*, *allium* being the old name for garlic, possibly derived from the Celtic *all*, meaning pungent.

Although chives were introduced into Britain by the Romans, they were not cultivated here until the Middle Ages. Yet the Chinese grew them 5,000 years ago, and used them not only in cooking but also in medicine, as an antidote to poisoning and a remedy for bleeding. Since then they have continued to play a small role in folk medicine because – like garlic and all its other relatives – chives are a good antiseptic. Being rich in iron, they are also good for anaemia, and since their action is diuretic they have been used to assist kidney function.

Chives are an excellent appetizer and digestive, and one of the most popular herbs to be used as a garnish. They enhance vegetable dishes, are delicious in omelettes, and versatile in sauces and salads. Chopped chives in cream cheese or butter are lovely with baked potatoes, and the little bulbs can be pickled in vinegar, like baby onions. The aroma of chives is destroyed with long cooking, so they are best added to hot dishes at the end of the cooking time.

Chives are a hardy perennial plant, found in the wild in a great variety of habitats, from dry rocky places to damp grassland and woodland edges. They are native to cool parts of Europe, and like a light, rich, damp soil best of all. Sow the seed in April for little clumps in the autumn. Cut them right back in the winter, and the following spring the leaves will grow from their cluster of little bulblets more thickly than ever.

If the leaves go yellow at the top give them some plant food, and lift and divide the clumps every three or four years. To keep the flavour in the leaves cut the mauve flower clusters throughout the summer (very pretty in a vase of mixed flowers and, like all the *allium* family, dry well for dried flower arrangements).

Chinese chives, *A. tuberosum*, have broader leaves, a coarser flavour, and dazzling white flowers.

Chives are a useful companion plant: if you plant them next to roses the latter never get black-spot. Chives grown near carrots discourage carrot fly, and near apple trees they will discourage apple scab.

CHIVE AND POTATO OMELETTE

In this omelette, waxy new potatoes combine with the delicious onion flavour of chives and a touch of soured cream to make a superlative filling. Food for a summer's day – easy to prepare, simply using the best ingredients in season.

8 oz (250 g) new potatoes, scrubbed
½ oz (15 g) butter, melted
2 tablespoons chopped chives
2 tablespoons soured cream
salt and pepper
6 eggs, beaten

Steam the potatoes for about 5 minutes. Cool them a little before cutting them into ¼ inch (5 mm) slices. Toss them in the melted butter until well coated, then mix in the chives and soured cream. Season with a little salt and pepper and keep warm.

Season the beaten eggs and make two omelettes in a lightly greased pan. As each one begins to set, put the potato and chive mixture on to one half of the omelette's surface and fold the other half over the top. Continue cooking until well set, and serve as soon as possible.

Serves 2

CORIANDER

Coriander is herb and spice rolled into one, and may well be man's oldest flavouring. About 5,000 years before Christ it was used in Oriental cookery, mentioned as a love-potion in *The Arabian Nights*, and also featured in Babylonian medicine.

In the Bible, coriander is one of the five plants designated as a bitter herb, ordained by God to be eaten by Jews at the feast of the Passover. Manna was 'like coriander seed, white; and the taste of it was like wafers made with honey'.

The Romans used coriander to flavour bread, and the Greeks cooked it with vegetables (still with us in the form of *à la Grecque*). It has always been popular in Eastern cookery, both the leaf and seed giving distinctive flavours to Indian, Chinese and Indonesian dishes. The leaves give a superlative flavour to sauces and soups, and are widely used as a garnish in Indian food. Coriander, ginger and garlic lend a unique taste to many Chinese dishes, particularly fish. The seeds are used in breads, cakes and biscuits, in liqueur manufacture and in confectionery.

Coriander was much used once as a beauty herb, especially for the skin. The water from an infusion would tone down a florid complexion, and in medieval times was used to clear a spotty face.

Coriander was one of Hippocrates' simples, and over the centuries it has been used to soothe the stomach and prevent griping. Chewing the seed stimulates the secretion of gastric juices, and coriander was still listed in the British Pharmacopoeia at the beginning of this century, to relieve internal pain.

Coriander, a native of the eastern Mediterranean, needs a light, rich soil and full sun, and will flourish in well-drained pots and window boxes. Sow the seed in the late spring, in drills about 1 inch (2.5 cm) deep. Germination can be slow, but when the plants are several inches tall, thin them out. At this stage they will smell quite unpleasant (coriander gets its name from the Greek for 'bed bug'), but as the plants mature they develop their pleasantly aromatic scent.

CORIANDER COMPLEXION WATER

1 medium bunch fresh coriander
hot water

Bruise the coriander leaves and put them into a saucepan. Cover with hot water, bring to the boil and simmer for 3 minutes, completely covered with a lid, then strain and cool completely. Store in an airtight jar and keep in a cool, dark place. Pat on the face using cotton wool.

COD WITH GINGER, GARLIC AND CORIANDER

Fresh green coriander leaves have an extraordinary, delicious flavour which is typical of much Oriental cookery. Here, in combination with ginger and garlic, it makes one of the best simple fish dishes that I know, served with fresh egg noodles.

4 cod steaks
salt and pepper
1/2 inch (1 cm) fresh root ginger, grated
2 cloves garlic, peeled and crushed
2 tablespoons sesame oil
a small bunch fresh coriander, chopped finely
fresh coriander leaves, to garnish

Season the cod steaks with salt and pepper. Mix the grated ginger and crushed garlic into the sesame oil and stir in the finely chopped coriander. Mix thoroughly to a paste, then place a quarter of the mixture on the top of each steak. Wrap in clingfilm and steam until cooked – about 6–8 minutes, depending on the thickness of the fish.

Allow to stand for 2 minutes off the heat, then unwrap and serve on warm plates, sprinkled with fresh coriander leaves.

Serves 4

NEW POTATOES IN SPICY CORIANDER SAUCE

This Indonesian inspired sauce is a most beautiful green colour. As well as tasting superb, potatoes are transformed with it.

1½ lb (750 g) new potatoes, scrubbed

For the sauce:
½ pint (300 ml) boiling water
2 tablespoons desiccated coconut
3 tablespoons dry-roasted peanuts
1 teaspoon coriander seeds
1 teaspoon ground turmeric
1 small bunch fresh coriander, chopped
1 oz (25 g) margarine
1 tablespoon flour

Pour the boiling water over the coconut and infuse for 15 minutes. Strain into the food processor and add the peanuts, spices and chopped coriander. Blend.

Melt the margarine over a gentle heat and stir in the flour. Gradually add the liquid and stir while the sauce thickens. Simmer gently for 5 minutes.

Boil or steam the potatoes until lightly cooked. Cut them in half, put them into a warm dish, and spoon the sauce over the top.

Serves 4

DILL

Also known as dill-weed, dill gets its name from the Anglo Saxon *dillan*, to lull or soothe, because of its stomach-soothing properties (dill is widely used in gripe water). Both leaves and seeds have been used since the earliest times for, like fennel and coriander, dill is herb and spice in one. It is mentioned in the Bible, in Egyptian texts, and was recommended by Greek and Roman physicians. By 1570 it was under cultivation in Britain, and the Pilgrim Fathers took it with them to America where it became known as 'Meetin' Seed' – dill seeds were given to children to chew during long Sunday sermons!

Dill was, so they say, used by witches in their spells, yet was also powerful against their evil mischief. Mostly it is a plant of good omen – English country brides used to wear a sprig of dill on their wedding day.

Dill is still often used in children's medicines, since it is good for minor digestive problems, including hiccups. Dill tea is recommended for a good night's sleep, for its soothing and sedative qualities.

Native to Southern Europe, dill is an annual or biennial member of the same family as parsley, and is now widely cultivated in Europe, India and North America. It grows to about 3 feet (90 cm) tall and has feathery leaves and large yellow umbels of flowers at midsummer. Although it will tolerate most soils, it prefers a warm position where it will often self-seed. The best way to grow dill is to sow the seeds in drills in the spring. It grows well next to cabbages, but not near carrots. And don't plant dill near fennel as they may cross-fertilize and the resulting plant will have neither the scent nor the flavour of either herb.

Dill is a characteristic flavouring in Scandinavian cooking, and is also popular in Turkey and Russia. It gives a beautiful taste to marinated herrings, and is also used in pickling gherkins. The seeds give their pungent flavour to cakes and pastries, traditionally served after a heavy meal to settle the stomach. The taste of the leaves is subtle and aromatic, delicious in soups, sauces and fish dishes, and in Poland they cook new potatoes and peas with dill weed in much the same way as we use mint. Fresh dill butter is lovely on baked potatoes.

GRAVLAX

When dill comes into season this is the best of all the many wonderful things you can do with this herb. Gravlax is, to my mind, better than the best smoked salmon: it makes a delicious starter on its own, or a superb main course dished up with a selection of sauces and cold vegetables.

1 lb (500 g) salmon fillet, sliced in half lengthways
4 tablespoons sugar
6 tablespoons salt
masses of freshly ground black pepper
a large bunch of fresh dill
finely chopped dill, to garnish

Put one half of the salmon fillet skin side down on a flat dish, spread with the sugar and salt mixed together, and sprinkle over lots of pepper. Place a generous quantity of dill on top, and cover with the other half salmon fillet, skin side up this time. Weight it down by putting a plate over the top and something fairly heavy on top of the plate. Put in the fridge, and turn twice a day for 3–4 days, basting with the liquids that ooze out.

To serve, skin the fish, and wipe it clean. Cut into very thin slivers, and sprinkle with fresh chopped dill.

Serves 4

PASTA BOWS WITH DILL PESTO

Pesto is traditionally made with basil, yet dill also makes a deliciously summery sauce, perfect for pasta. Serve this dish with chilled white wine and a tossed salad of crisp lettuce, radicchio, fennel and tomato.

4–6 tablespoons olive oil
1 small bunch fresh dill, chopped
2 cloves of garlic, crushed
1½ oz (40 g) pine nuts
1 oz (25 g) grated Parmesan
12 oz (350 g) pasta bows, cooked 'al dente'

Put the olive oil, dill, garlic and pine nuts into the food processor and blend to a purée. Stir in the grated Parmesan. Leave to stand while the pasta bows are cooking.

Drain the cooked pasta thoroughly, then toss in the dill sauce. Serve immediately on warm plates, with crusty bread and the salad on the side.

Serves 4

FENNEL

The ancient Greeks crowned the winners of the Olympic games with a wreath of fennel. They called it *marathon*, after a word meaning 'to grow thin', because it was believed that fennel prevents the body from putting on fat. Its aniseed taste certainly diminishes the appetite and, because it allays hunger pangs, it was one of the herbs allowed on fasting days, and so became a sacred herb.

In the 'Language of Flowers' fennel came to characterize strength, because gladiators apparently mixed it with their food to build themselves up. Greek athletes were also known to take it for stamina as well as for courage, and as a guard against overweight.

The ancient Greeks believed that knowledge came to man from Olympus in the form of a fiery coal contained in a fennel stalk, and in folklore it is generally thought of as a protective herb, warding off witchcraft. It was dedicated to St John and woven into garlands to hang over doorways on the eve of 24 June, his feast day, and sprigs of fennel hung from the rafters would, it was believed, drive evil spirits out of a house.

Fennel was one of Hippocrates' simples, and was used for centuries in slimming diets. Like dill, it is also a constituent of gripe water since it relieves cramps. In country medicine fennel had a reputation for strengthening the eyesight, and infusions of fennel seeds were used in eyewashes.

A hardy perennial, fennel will grow on poor soils so long as it is well-drained and in a sunny position. The herb is closely related to Florence fennel which is cultivated for its swollen stem base and makes a delicious vegetable. Fennel, the herb, grows up to 8 feet (2.4 metres) tall and has flat umbels of yellow flowers in the summer.

Fennel has been a culinary herb for at least 2,000 years – both leaves and seeds are used, especially in fish dishes. It is also excellent with egg, potato and cheese recipes, and try adding fennel seeds to an apple pie. Highly aromatic, the seeds have been much used in perfumery and in the manufacture of liqueurs. Fennel leaves were popular as a strewing herb in Elizabethan times.

RED MULLET WITH FENNEL

Fresh fennel is proverbially good with fish of all sorts, and this recipe for red mullet is no exception. The delicate flavour of the fish is enchanced by cooking it with a sprig of fennel inside it, and the mullet is then served with an aromatic fennel sauce.

1 head Florence fennel, separated into 'leaves'
1/2 pint (300 ml) béchamel sauce
5 tablespoons single cream
sea salt and pepper
a small bunch fennel leaves, snipped
4 medium red mullet
4 large sprigs fennel
olive oil

Boil the Florence fennel for 12–15 minutes, or until thoroughly softened, then cool a little and chop roughly. Mix into the béchamel sauce and liquidize to a purée in the food processor. Stir in the cream and season to taste. Stir in the fennel leaves.

Wipe the red mullet and insert a sprig of fennel into each one. Sprinkle with sea salt and brush with olive oil. Grill until well cooked through – about 5 minutes on each side. Warm the sauce through over a very low heat for 5 minutes, then serve with the fish.

Serves 4

HYSSOP

In the Bible the Temple was purged with hyssop, hyssop was used in the ritual cleansing of lepers, and it was offered to Christ, with vinegar, as he suffered on the Cross. It was a powerful herb against witchcraft and the powers of darkness, and was used in folk medicine as a chest herb, especially for pleurisy and bronchitis. It is powerfully antiseptic and was also a wound herb. Both butterflies and bees are attracted to hyssop, which contributes to a superb honey. With its enchanting violet-blue flowers it was used as a hedging plant in Elizabethan gardens, and modern strains produce lovely flowers of pink, red and white. Used sparingly in cooking because of its bitterness, it contributes flavour in the manufacture of spirits and liqueurs such as *absinthe* and Chartreuse.

LAVENDER

Lavender has been an established garden plant in England since the 12th century, grown by monks in infirmary gardens and by householders in their kitchen gardens. It was grown for its inimitable perfume, traditionally used to scent baths and washing water (the name lavender comes from the Latin *lavare*, to wash). Dried lavender has been used in aromatics for centuries too. The only use of the herb in cooking is that the young leaves are delicious in salads, and the young shoots a pleasant addition to stew.

By the 17th century it was a popular household commodity, used to perfume linen – it also kept moths away – and, as it possessed valuable antiseptic qualities, it was strewn on the floors of houses and churches to ward off disease.

Lavender-growing became a commercial enterprise in the early 19th century, notably at Hitchin in Hertfordshire, where an acre of lavender was said to yield from 12–30 lb (5.5–13.5 kg) of essential oil. Yardley had a flourishing soap and perfumery industry in London, based on their lavender fields at Mitcham. Although no longer grown there, Mitcham lavender is still world famous, and has left a legacy of street names in that part of London: Lavender Rise, Hill, Gardens, Grove, Terrace and many others. It was a common sight to see 'Herb Women' selling bunches of lavender from their barrows on the streets of London.

Lavender was used medicinally for its antiseptic properties – a lotion was applied to cuts and bruises, wounds and burns. The oil was rubbed into children's hair to kill lice and their eggs.

Lavender oil has a soothing and sedative quality, and is used to settle stomach disorders as well as being an important ingredient of smelling salts. Lavender pickers used to put a sprig of lavender under their hats to prevent them from getting a headache in the hot harvest sunshine, and lavender tea was a popular remedy for insomnia.

There are numerous varieties of lavender, including a white one. It is a perennial shrub growing on a woody stem and thrives on poor, well-drained soils. The flowers are best harvested just before they open in the middle of the summer. Lavender is a good companion plant for vegetables – it makes them healthier and gives them a better flavour.

LAVENDER *POT POURRI*

There is something special about the fragrant scent of *pot-pourri* as you walk into a room, and it is very simple to make. If you don't dry your own flowers they can be bought from various stockists and chemists. This recipe is a particularly aromatic one – it uses orange blossom as well as lavender and rose petals, and I like to scent it with sandalwood and orange peel. The orris root powder is added as a fixture to help the fragrances last longer, and is available from most chemists.

1 cup lavender buds
1/2 cup dried rose petals
1/2 cup orange blossoms
1 cup mixed herbs (sweet marjoram, thyme, rosemary
*   and sage)*
a little grated orange rind
a drop or two of essential oil of sandalwood
2 tablespoons orris root powder

Mix the lavender, rose petals, orange blossoms and herbs together and stir well. Add the grated orange rind and essential oil and stir again. Finally stir in the orris root powder and your *pot-pourri* is ready.

MARIGOLD

'Mary Golds' were dedicated by medieval folk to the Virgin Mary, in the belief that she wore one pinned to her robe. Marigolds have been used in medicine since the times of the ancient Greeks, and were a sacred flower in Hindu temples: they are still used today in Indian religious and festive rituals. The marigold's healing qualities included the ability to bring down inflamed lymph glands, and to treat duodenal ulcers. Externally it was used as a skin lotion to heal damaged tissue, and also as an eye lotion. Marigold petals make a spicy addition to a summer salad, and give both zest and a lovely golden colour to rich dishes – a poor man's saffron!

MARJORAM

The Greeks believed that Aphrodite created marjoram: she took it from the waters of the ocean to the top of the highest mountains where it now grows close to the rays of the sun. To them it was symbolic of peace and happiness, and this is reflected in a local Somerset name for marjoram, 'joy of the mountain'. Another story goes that the herb is named after Amaracus, a Greek youth in the service of Cinyres, King of Cyprus. He accidentally broke a vase of perfume and was so terrified of the consequences that he fell unconscious to the ground. The gods in their mercy took pity on him and changed him into the herb that bears his name.

Marjoram was an important herb to the Tudors who planted it in their knot gardens and mazes, and it became such an indispensable commodity that the pioneers of the early 17th century took it with them to the New World. Little pots of marjoram were a fashionable sight standing on 18th-century windowsills, and it was also used in nosegays and as a strewing herb.

Marjoram has had its uses in folk medicine. Generally speaking it is a good tonic and settling herb – it soothes the stomach and revives sluggish organs. One herbalist maintained that to smell wild marjoram frequently was enough to keep a person in good health! An infusion of the flowers was a folk remedy for seasickness.

An infusion of marjoram is good for sore throats, a blocked-up nose and a cough. Sweetened with honey it is a soothing tisane to calm irritability and get rid of a nervous headache. It is said that inhaling the vapours from the juice will help relieve a migraine.

Marjoram oil was believed to be good for rheumatism, and comforting for stiff joints. Country people made a poultice of powdered marjoram to cure a toothache, and also put it in their ears to relieve earache. Some folk believe that marjoram allays nightmares and checks bedwetting.

Marjoram is a pungent herb and much used in cookery, particularly to flavour roast meats and pâtés. It is an excellent herb for a marinade and an important ingredient of a *bouquet garni*. Its strong flavour is often used to spice sausages and stuffings. The chopped leaves are delicious tossed in butter and cooked slowly with cubed potatoes, and it is a superb herb for pizzas and pasta dishes. It dries very well and is one of the herbs traditionally used in sleep pillows, nosegays and sachets. It was, so they say, the favourite strewing herb of Elizabeth I.

MARJORAM SCONES

Warm herby scones, served with butter when fresh from the oven, are one of the most delightful of summer treats. As they are cooking, the aroma of dried marjoram fills the kitchen with its sweetness. I have never known any leftovers from this recipe!

8 oz (250 g) flour
a pinch of salt
4 oz (100 g) margarine
3 teaspoons baking powder
1 tablespoon dried marjoram
milk

Sift the flour with the salt. Rub the margarine into the flour and then add the baking powder. Stir in the marjoram and mix to a light dough with a little milk. Knead well, then roll out to about ½ inch (1 cm) thick and cut into rounds with a cutter or glass. Bake on a greased baking tray at 450°F/230°C/Gas 8 for 10–12 minutes until well risen and golden on top. Cool on a rack, and eat while still warm.

Makes 10

MINT

Mint's botanical name '*pulegium*' comes from the Latin *pulex*, a flea, because fresh mint was used as a flea-deterrent and also to eradicate other insects. It has become a symbol of virtue because of its cleansing properties, and was used in various ways in folk medicine. Mint tea was prescribed for a cold, and a decoction of mint was recommended as a wash for sore mouths. The tea was also found to be good for nervous headaches and agitation, and was believed to recharge energy and act as a tonic. It was widely considered to be aphrodisiac, and its antiseptic qualities made it an effective treatment for cuts and skin rashes.

Mint is mentioned in the Bible as a tithe, and was one of the bitter herbs to be eaten with the Paschal lamb. The Athenians used to rub their arms with it and put it into baths to refresh and strengthen the body. The Romans would scour a banqueting table with mint before a feast, and strew the floor with the herb to stimulate guests' appetites. Wayward women in Roman times made a mint paste with honey to disguise the scent on their breath after drinking wine – forbidden by law and punishable by death.

The creeping mint pennyroyal used to be grown in little pots for taking on long sea voyages; its cleansing and antiseptic properties were used to purify stale water.

Mint is an appetizer and digestive. Mint sauce was a Roman invention, a good foil for strong and indigestible meats like lamb. Mint butter is delicious on chops, and mint leaves finely chopped are a refreshing finishing touch to a salad. A sprig of mint is traditionally added to a saucepan of peas or new potatoes while they are cooking, and the peppermint flavour also lends itself to desserts, such as sorbet and chocolate mousse. Mint is a classic addition to drinks such as fruit punches and Pimms.

'Plant a little mint, madam, then step out of the way so you don't get hurt,' as the gardener said to the lady of the house. The best way to grow mint so that it does not take over is to plant it in old sinks or plastic buckets which you then dig into the earth, or to enclose the roots with roofing tiles or slates. Propagate it from root runners, give it a damp, shady place, and all it will need is a transplant every three years or so to regenerate its strength.

MINTED CHOCOLATE MOUSSE

The addition of fresh mint to a rich chocolate mousse is to my mind a great improvement – it makes it less cloying, and lingers on the palate deliciously. It adds a note of sophistication to a classic dessert.

4 oz (100 g) plain chocolate
1 oz (25 g) butter, softened
4 eggs, separated
2 sprigs mint, finely chopped

Break the chocolate into squares and melt in a bowl with the softened butter over simmering water. Beat the egg yolks thoroughly and, off the heat, stir into the melted chocolate. Stir in the chopped mint. Beat the egg whites very stiffly and fold them into the mixture. Pour into little pots or glasses, and put in the fridge for 2–3 hours until ready to serve.

Serves 4–6

PARSLEY

The ancient Greeks believed that parsley sprang from the blood of Archemorus, the forerunner of death. According to legend he was carelessly laid by his nurse in a bed of parsley and was eaten by serpents, so to them parsley was associated with death and funerals. In later times, Christians dedicated parsley to St Peter when he succeeded Charon as guide to the dead. The Greeks had a tradition of placing a wreath of parsley on graves and they even had a saying, 'He has need now of nothing but a little parsley', meaning that 'He is dead and just needs a parsley wreath on his tomb.'

Curiously enough, parsley was also a symbol of strength to the Greeks. Hercules was said to have chosen parsley as a garland, and the winner of the Nemean games was crowned with a similar garland. Homer tells that chariot horses were fed on parsley, and the Romans gave it to gladiators before a fight. Garlands of parsley were worn at feasts to absorb fumes and prevent drunkenness, both by the Greeks and by the Romans.

Parsley's long germination period is due to the fact that the seed, so the old wives' tale goes, must go to the Devil and back seven times before it will grow. So plant your parsley on Good Friday to ensure safe germination! It is said to be very bad luck to transplant parsley, especially from a house you are moving out of to the new garden. Never chop parsley when you are in love because your love will die, and if you dream of parsley you will be crossed in love.

Both the root and the seed of parsley are to be found in European pharmocopoeias. Its essential oil is used in the treatment of malaria and associated maladies, and is also an excellent aid to digestion. It has been used to regulate menstruation, and the roots have been used to cure inflammation of the kidneys.

Parsley is highly nutritious and contains vitamins A, B and C, large amounts of iron and calcium, and many mineral salts – so it probably does you more good than the food it is used to decorate! It is a versatile and much used herb in cooking – but take heed of a Spanish proverb: if you eat too much parsley you will look older than your years!

Parsley is a biennial, but the flavour of its leaves is best in the first year. It likes partial shade in a warm, moist, rich soil which has been worked to a fine tilth. Thin out carefully as it grows, since the plants require space.

MUSSELS WITH PARSLEY AND GARLIC BUTTER

This is a delectable way of serving mussels – in the half shell, covered with a parsley and garlic butter, and baked until piping hot. Delicious as a starter, with warm, fresh bread.

6 pints (3.5 litres) mussels, scrubbed
4 oz (100 g) butter
3 large cloves garlic, peeled and crushed
a medium bunch parsley, finely chopped
salt and pepper
2 tablespoons dried breadcrumbs

Put the mussels into a large saucepan, cover, and open them over a gentle heat, shaking the pan from time to time. Remove them from their shells and put each one into a half shell. Melt the butter, and stir in the crushed garlic. Stand over a very low heat for 5 minutes, then add the parsley and stir thoroughly. Simmer gently for a further 5 minutes, then leave to stand for a minute or two. Season to taste with salt and pepper.

Spoon a little of this garlic butter on top of each mussel in its shell, then sprinkle with the breadcrumbs. Bake in a preheated oven at 375°F/190°C/Gas 5 for 10 minutes, and serve sizzling hot.

Serves 4

ROSEMARY

Rosemary is *ros maris*, dew of the sea, because it grows on the shores of the Mediterranean within reach of the sea spray. Its mist-blue flowers are the colour of the sea, too, and there is also a legend that they got their colour from the blue cloak of the Virgin Mary when, during the flight into Egypt, she threw it over a rosemary bush to dry. Up until then the flowers had been white.

The Pharaohs had a sprig of rosemary put in their tombs to sweeten their journey to the hereafter, and the Romans believed that it brought happiness to the living and peace to the dead. To symbolize fidelity and friendship, gilded sprigs of rosemary were often inserted into a bridal bouquet. Rosemary is traditionally the herb of remembrance, and Greek students wore a rosemary garland in the belief that it increased the blood supply to the brain and helped the memory. They say that rosemary grows only in the gardens of the righteous, and that where it thrives the woman is the boss in the household!

Rosemary is a powerful antiseptic and was used as a disinfectant in public places in days of pestilence and plague. The posy carried by the monarch at the Maundy Thursday ceremony, while presenting money to the poor, contained sprigs of rosemary and thyme, both good antiseptics, to protect the sovereign from infection.

The essential oil of rosemary is good for neuralgia, rheumatism, gout and kidney trouble. Infusions of the herb are good for the heart and for blood circulation, and will combat anaemia and depression. Rosemary is also a cleansing wound herb.

Rosemary has a strong flavour and is excellent in barbecue cookery, in marinades and stuffings. It gives pungency to aromatic jams and jellies, and makes wonderful scones. It is always included in a *bouquet garni*, and is a traditional garnish for a claret cup. It has also been much used in perfumery and incense, and was an important strewing herb as well as being used in *pot-pourri*.

There are many varieties of rosemary, including a rare white one. The plant requires a well-drained soil and a warm, sheltered position – and it does well next to sage. It requires very little water and will flourish on the poorest of soils, preferring lime. Although a perennial evergreen, it dislikes cold winters and needs protection from wind and frost. It can also be grown as a pot plant.

ROSEMARY HERB BATH

Tie either fresh or dried rosemary in a muslin bag and hang it under the hot tap whilst the bath is running. Alternatively soak the bag in the bath while you are in it yourself.

MARINADE FOR LEG OF LAMB

2 pints (1.2 litres) red wine
1/4 pint (150 ml) white wine vinegar
1/4 pint (150 ml) olive oil
a large bunch fresh thyme
several good sprigs rosemary
6 bay leaves
1 tablespoon each salt and black peppercorns

Mix all the ingredients together and pour them over the leg of lamb in a dish. Turn the meat in the marinade 3 or 4 times a day for 4–5 days at room temperature (6–8 days if refrigerated). Drain off the marinade, wipe the joint dry and roast it in the usual way.

RUE

Rue is the herb of sorrow and remorse, a bitter herb associated with repentance. Yet it has played an important part in the long history of healing: it was used in ancient Chinese medicine as an antidote to malarial poisoning, and was a traditional treatment for epilepsy. It has been used over the centuries for the relief of menstrual pain and disorders of the nervous system, but its best known use was as an eye lotion – the Romans believed it had the power to confer second sight as well!

Mithradates, King of Pontus from 120–63 BC, was a toxicologist who sought a single antidote to every known poison. A well-kept secret until his death, his final invincible formula was discovered to be two dried figs, two nuts, and twenty leaves of rue pounded and mixed with a grain of salt!

In 1760 a rumour in the City of London that the plague had broken out at St Thomas' Hospital sent the price of rue rocketing in Covent Garden market: by the following day it had risen by 40 per cent! As well as being widely used in times of pestilence, rue was also strewn in the Law Courts to protect the judiciary from gaol fever, and it was included in the nosegay traditionally carried by judges in court.

Rue was fastened over a door to prevent witches from entering, and in medieval times a little bag containing dried rue leaves was believed to be a powerful charm against witchcraft.

Rue leaves, with their deeply indented club-shape, are the model for the club in playing cards, and also feature in heraldry. Sprigs of rue are interlaced on the collar of the Order of the Thistle (thistle-and-rue = thistle andrew, patron saint of Scotland). The herb, which has no culinary value, has various other uses: the oil is used in perfumery, and rue tea will kill fleas, and also clear a spotty complexion!

They say that rue grows best when stolen from a neighbouring garden. It likes a well-drained limestone soil and a sheltered position in full sun. It is an aromatic semi-evergreen shrub with a mousy, stale smell and a bitter taste. Its foliage colour is a pretty blueish green, and it bears little yellow flowers which last through the summer into autumn.

SAGE

Sage's generic name, *salvia*, comes from the Latin *salvere*, to be in good health. Because of its powerful medicinal properties, it was considered by many as a universal healer of all ills. It was used to treat lung conditions, fever, liver disease, respiratory tract infections, and open wounds. Its antiseptic properties were used to combat the plague – sage juice with vinegar was a popular remedy. It was generally believed to be good for the brain – the ancient Greeks found that it slowed down the diminution of the senses, declining faculties and failing memory. This belief lingered into the 18th century when Culpeper recommended sage tea to sharpen the mind and improve the memory.

The Greeks drink sage tea to this day, a habit taken up at one point in history by the Chinese – they preferred it to their own China tea, and carried on a barter trade with the Dutch, exchanging sage tea for three times the weight of their own product!

The Romans called sage *herba sacra* and dedicated it to Jupiter: they gathered it with special ceremonial, in white tunics and bare feet, having first offered sacrifices of bread and wine. They brought it to Britain where it grows freely both in the wild and as a garden plant. It likes a well-drained, chalky soil, and a sunny position. There are many varieties, some red-leaved, some variegated, but the common sage has downy grey-green leaves and violet-blue flowers which attract clouds of bees in the summer. It grows particularly well near rosemary and rue, and repels cabbage fly.

'Sage the Saviour' was believed to prolong life: 'He that would live for aye must eat sage in May.' A thriving sage bush indicated a thriving family fortune, and it flourished or withered according to the prosperity of the master of the house. Yet where sage does prosper in the garden the woman was said to rule the roost, and nervous men were reported as cutting down flourishing sage bushes in case they were mocked by their neighbours!

Sage is an excellent herb for cooking, famous as a good companion for pork in a sage and onion stuffing. It is delicious in sauces and butters, and a cheese omelette with sage is something special. Various English cheeses are made with sage, as in Gloucester and Derby, and eels are traditionally stewed with sage. The herb dries very well, and can be used through the winter months in stews and casseroles, or sprinkled over pizzas.

MUSHROOMS EN COCOTTE

Little cocotte dishes of garlicky mushrooms flavoured with sage make a delicious starter to a meal. Serve with fresh warm bread to mop up the juices.

12 oz (350 g) small button mushrooms
2 oz (50 g) butter
2 large cloves garlic, peeled and crushed
2 tablespoons finely chopped sage
1 oz (25 g) fresh breadcrumbs
vegetable oil for frying

Steam the mushrooms until cooked through, about 3 minutes, then remove the stalks. Melt the butter and stir in the garlic and sage. Cook over a gentle heat for 2–3 minutes. Chop the stalks finely and add them to the sage butter. Fry the breadcrumbs separately in very hot oil until golden and crisp. Drain on kitchen paper and keep warm.

To assemble, put the mushrooms into four cocotte dishes and pour the mushroom and herb butter over the top. Sprinkle with the fried breadcrumbs and heat through in a very hot oven for 5 minutes. Serve at once.

Serves 4

SAGE BUTTER WITH BABY ONIONS

Sage has a famous affinity with onions, as in sage and onion stuffing that goes so well with the Christmas turkey or a Sunday joint of pork. So it comes as no surprise that sage butter should be delicious with boiled baby onions – a scrumptious side dish for grilled or roast meat.

1 small bunch fresh sage, chopped very finely
3 oz (75 g) butter, melted
1¼ lb (600 g) small onions, peeled

Stir the chopped sage into the melted butter and simmer gently for 5 minutes. Leave on the side to stand while the onions are cooking.

Cover the onions with boiling water and simmer them for 10–15 minutes until very tender. Drain them thoroughly and put into a warm dish. Pour the sage butter over the top, toss them, and they are ready to serve.

Serves 4

THYME

Thyme has grown over the slopes of Mount Hymettus ever since the times of classical Greece, and the honey from it is unrivalled in fragrance. The Greeks used to burn thyme as incense in their temples, and indeed its name comes from their word for incense. The herb, to them, represented the graceful elegance of the Attic style, and to 'smell of thyme' was praise bestowed on writers who had mastered it. There is a legend that tells how thyme sprang up from the tears of Helen of Troy.

Thyme is the herb of the fairies, a favourite haunt of elves, and it was maintained by country folk that tufts of thyme growing in wild places were the play-

grounds of the 'wee folk'. Thyme is also associated with strength and happiness, and was a symbol of courage and strength.

Thyme has had a multitude of medicinal uses throughout history. The Romans used it as a remedy for melancholy, and it was generally thought to be good for lethargy and depression. Thyme tisane calms the nerves and gives a good night's sleep, and is also good for headaches, coughs, catarrh and asthma. It has been used in folk medicine for whooping cough and bronthitis.

Thyme is a powerful antiseptic and was a protection against leprosy and the plague. It makes a disinfectant gargle and mouthwash, and a good poultice for wounds. Thyme vinegar is said to cure a headache, and a sprig of thyme in the bath relieves fatigue.

Thyme is one of the great classic culinary herbs, unequalled for flavouring meat dishes and stews. Its strong flavour permeates marinating foods, is superb in wine cookery, and goes well with rich foods since it is a good digestive. Lemon thyme is delicious in custards and fruit desserts, and thyme is one of the herbs used to flavour Benedictine.

There are numerous varieties of thyme, of various colours and habits. They all like a well-drained, sandy soil or loam, and thrive on sunny slopes in dry, rocky places. Thyme will grow between paving stones, and in pots and window boxes as well as in garden beds. Divide old plants every three or four years as they tend to get straggly and lose their fragrance.

THYME SLEEP PILLOW

Choose pretty fabric made of pure cotton or silk – man-made fibres have a staling effect on the fragrance of herbs over a period of time. Select fabrics with a fine weave so that small leaves cannot escape, and perhaps use some old lace to edge the pillow with.

Cut the fabric about 12 × 10 inches (30 × 25 cm), so that with a seam allowance of ½ inch (1 cm), the final pillow will measure 10 × 8 inches (25 × 20 cm). With the right sides together machine up three sides, leaving the fourth side open. Trim the seam allowance and turn right side out. Press carefully.

For the filling, take a few handfuls of dried thyme, and mix with some lavender buds, some lemon verbena leaves and some hops – all dried. Rosemary flowers keep nightmares away, so they say, so add a few of these too. Marjoram is soothing and sedative so this herb is often added to a sleep pillow. I like to add a little ground allspice just for extra exotic fragrance, and finally a tablespoon or two of orris root powder to fix the scents. Mix all these together thoroughly, and fill the pillow with it. Stitch up the open side neatly, and edge with lace if desired. Slip the herb pillow inside your pillowcase. Sweet dreams!

SUMMER THYME SALAD

A dreadful pun, but the title more or less describes the contents of a delectable and elegant fruit salad. The addition of fresh thyme is an unusual touch, which enhances the summer flavours and gives fragrance to a memorable dessert.

4 greengages, stoned
12 oz (350 g) cherries, stoned
8 oz (250 g) strawberries, hulled
4 peaches, stoned
half a melon, balled
2 tablespoons fresh thyme, chopped finely
1/2 pint (300 ml) fresh orange juice

To decorate:
sprigs of flowering thyme

Slice all the prepared fruits – the greengages, cherries, strawberries and peaches. Mix with the melon balls and put into a large glass dish.

Sprinkle the chopped thyme over the top, pour on the juice and mix thoroughly. Chill for several hours, and serve decorated with sprigs of flowering thyme.

Serves 6

OTHER TITLES IN THE SERIES

The Little Green Avocado Book
The Little Garlic Book
The Little Pepper Book
The Little Lemon Book
The Little Apple Book
The Little Strawberry Book
The Little Mustard Book
The Little Honey Book
The Little Nut Book
The Little Mushroom Book
The Little Bean Book
The Little Rice Book
The Little Tea Book
The Little Coffee Book
The Little Chocolate Book
The Little Curry Book
The Little Mediterranean Food Book
The Little Exotic Vegetable Book
The Little Exotic Fruit Book
The Little Yoghurt Book
The Little Tofu Book
The Little Breakfast Book
The Little Egg Book
The Little Potato Book
The Little Spice Book